My Goals Vision Board

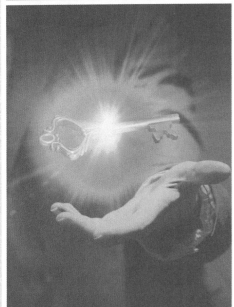

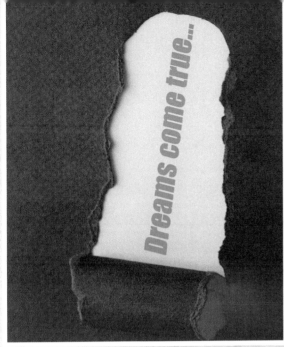

Personal Development

INVESTING IN YOURSELF

BIG CHANGE

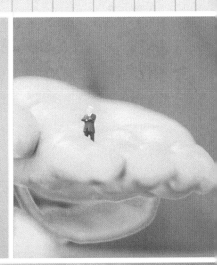

EMPOWER YOURSELF

I CAN'T

THE RIGHT WAY

cAREER

RONG WAY

RIGHT WAY

Professional Goals

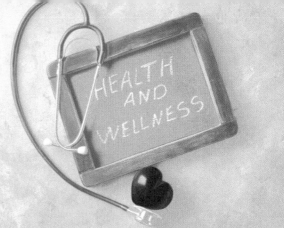

Health and Wellness

HEALTHY LIFESTYLE

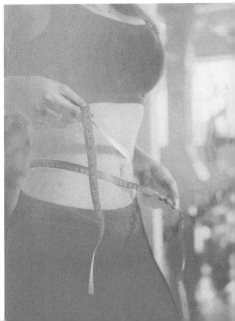

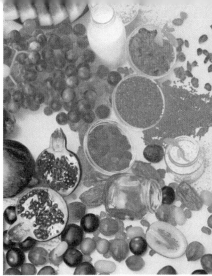

Relationships

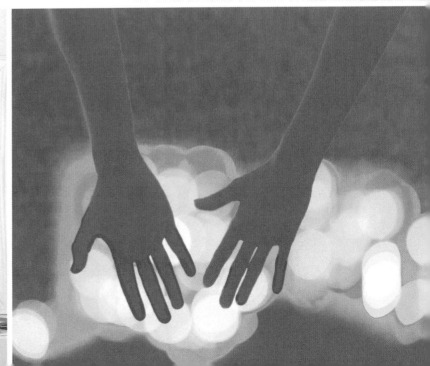

Relationship

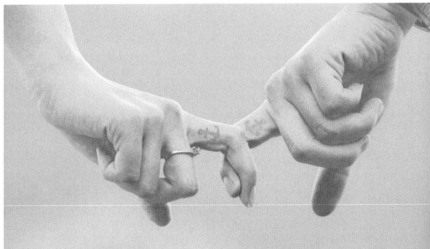

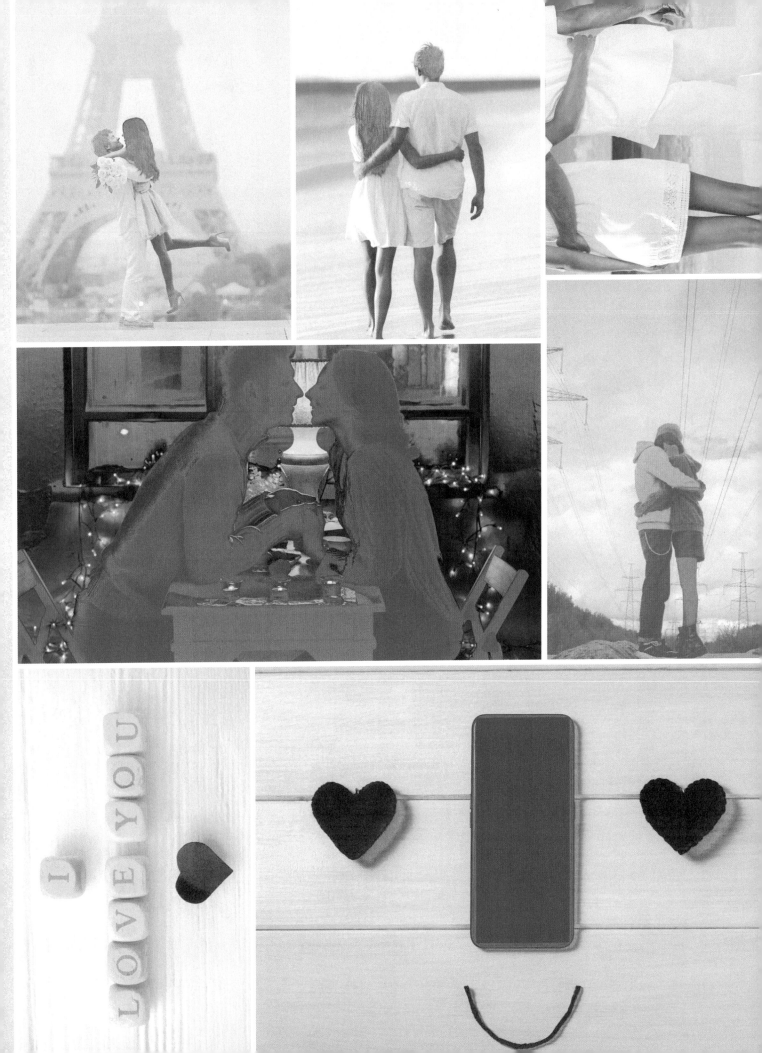

Travel and Adventure

YES TO
NEW
ADVENTURES
→

CHANGE OF
SCENERY
→

E X P L O R E

Financial Success

SOLUTION

STRATEGY

$

DREAMS
+
WORK
=
────────
SUCCESS

Creativity and Hobbies

UPDATE STRATEGY

TIME TO THINK CREATIVE

Education and Learning

NEW MINDSET

LOADING...

MINDSET

YES
YOU
CAN

change your
mindset
and the results will
follow

Spirituality and Mindset

NEXT LEVEL

LOADING...

CHANGE YOUR MINDSET

Mindset

#business #process #innovative
#inspiration #investment #cooperation
#world #global #responsibility

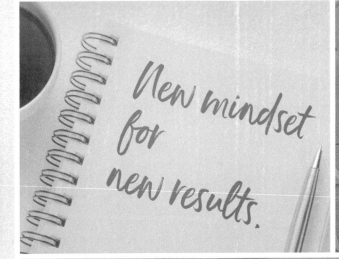

TRANSFORMATION LOADING...

Mindset

New mindset for new results.

mindset

CHANGE YOUR MINDSET

YOU CAN DO THIS

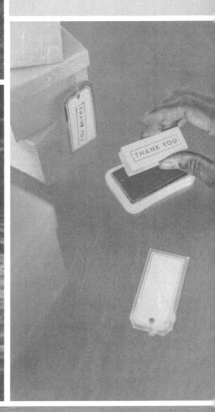

TRUST *the* PROCESS

I CAN -and- I WILL

never stop trying

trust your JOURNEY

you are AMAZING

Motivational Stickers

You are DOING GREAT

Be Happy

Thank You

FAMILY is FOREVER

make it happen

• I am • CONFIDENT

YES you CAN

Be Better

Motivational Stickers

DON'T STOP UNTIL YOU'RE PROUD

MINDSET IS EVERYTHING

I CAN AND I WILL WATCH ME

FAITH IT TILL YOU MAKE IT

NO Pain NO GAIN

Be Your Best

WORK for it

TODAY is the DAY

TAKE the RISK

Motivational Stickers

MAKE Today Great

Fresh START

Enjoy Life

I am HEALTHY

I am SUCCESSFUL

Made in the USA
Las Vegas, NV
23 January 2024

84789779R00040